"STANDING ON THE PROMISES OF GOD"

Inspirational Spoken Word for 366 days of the year

Author, Meliza C. Woodward
Whisper of Faith Publishing Company Inc.

Copyright © 2009 by Meliza C. Woodward
All rights reserved throughout the world.

Published by Meliza C. Woodward & Tarjatta Rose,
Whisper of Faith Publishing Company division of TakeHeed Ministry & Productions Inc.
Atlanta, Georgia www.takeheed333@yahoo.com

Compiled and Edited by Durinda Dickerson, & Minister Erica Dickerson

Cover Concept by Prophetess, Meliza C.Woodward

Designed Pictures by Tarjatta Rose-Johnson, Maxine Hopkins, Loretta Thompson-Hinton, Bobby Peoples, Renee Warren-Peoples

Other Scripture references are from the following sources:

"Scripture taken from the New American Standard Bible. Copyright 1960,1962,1963,1968,1971,1972,1973,1975,1975,1977,1995 by the Lockman Foundation, Used by permission."

Scripture taken from the Holy Bible, New International Version Copyright ©1973,1978,1984,by International Bible Society. Used by permission of Zondervan. All rights reserved.

Reproduction of text in whole or in part without the express written consent of the author is not permitted and is unlawful according to the 1976 United States Copyright Act. All rights reserved.

ISBN: 1442169753

EAN-13: 9781442169753

Printed in the United States of America.

DEDICATION

I Dedication this book to my wonderful daughter *Tarjatta Rose-Johnson* whom been my strength when I'm weak, along with my little angel granddaughter Ariel. Special thanks to my husband & step-children whom taught me to draw closer to the Lord, Thanks!
I am so thankful for my *Mother Ruby Herron-Woodward* whom raised me to love the Lord, she spend many nights praying over me to come through many valley and mountain top experiences. Praise God for my mother whom I love so very dearly. I love you, Grandmother *Sittie Mae Herron* who taught me to become the prayer warrior I am today.
I dedicate my first book to my Awesome siblings and their families, *James, Tanya, Timeko,* who been there to encourage me alone the way. They have always treated me like a mother figure being the eldest of 4; they used to call me Ms. Mulgillacutty, school teacher..
I also dedicate this book to my other brothers and sister afar, *Sister Angel Johnson*, Mounds, Ill. *Brother Peter Woodward* and 3 nephews in London, Brother *Teddy Woodward*, and Sister, *Sheila Woodward* in Harrisburg, Pa. I love you all so dearly with all my heart.
Special Thanks: I am so thankful for those who where my strength to up-hold me up when my marriage was falling apart, they were my shoulder

to cry on, **Ms. Erica** open her house to serve me like a Queen. I am so thankful for you *Minister Erica Dickerson* for believing in me and helping me complete the Vision God gave me with the help of *Loretta Thompson, Durinda Dickerson & Kia Dickerson, Pastor James & Minister Jackie Wright, all my TPN1 Family, Bobby & Renee People, and my special Prayer Warriors: Aunt Stella Williams, Apostle Katrina Hawkins, Keisha Copeland, Charlotte Childs, and many others.* I, Praise God for the **10 Mighty Warriors** whom answered the call to help do a month that would bless so many people. We all will share later in the book some Testimony we went through to get this Powerful Book ready for the Nations.
You are Worth it!

This book shall be dedicated to those whom I love so dearly, has passed on to Glory with our Heavenly Father, I pray we will see each other again!
My daughter, Karjatta Woodward-Rose , My Son, Sunjatta Woodward- Rose
Father James T. Woodward, Grandfather Robert Herron
Grandfather Theodore Woodward, Auntie Robbie Herron-Wilkins.

I Meliza has had many ups and down to endure, I made it only by the Grace of God' Love and Mercy. I have many hurts, pains, but I have learned all these things are working together for my good only to make me stronger.

This is just the beginning of what the Lord is doing with me, I have a lot to say to this hurting world, I want to encourage others to keep going, never give-up. Tomorrow is another day to see the Glory of what Our God has in store for us, the Sun will Shine again, storms will blow, but know this, Our God is in control of them all. We must learn not to just read the Word, but trust and live the Word. Our God Word does promise that He will watch over His Word, it shall come to pass if we believe and live according to His Word. Keep the Faith, the Best is yet to come for me and you! Finally, the most important one of all, is my Lord and Savior Jesus Christ, who raised me in this latter time to speak His Word with Boldness and Truth in Love to all mankind. I never thought the Lord would use me like this in this hour. Fixing our eyes on Jesus, the author and perfecter of our Faith, endure the suffering of the cross during your Journey! ***"Jesus will be waiting on you"***
Hebrews 12:2

Daughter of Zion, Meliza Woodward

CONTENTS

January	By Meliza Woodward	Page 7
February	By Tarjatta Rose – Johnson	Page 16
March	By Sharon Bacchus	Page 23
April	By Unisha Marshall	Page 32
May	By Ann St. Bernard	Page 42
June	By Tanya Woodward – Hadley	Page 51
July	By Timeko Woodard – Huntley	Page 59
August	By Dianne Causey	Page 67
September	By Meliza Woodward	Page 76
October	By James Woodward	Page 84
November	By Carolyn James	Page 92
December	By Shirley Hayden	Page 101

Conclusion: Special Prayer..........Page 113

Other Materials..........Page 115

Journal Notes..........Page 117

January
Restoration Shall Come to your House
Acts 1:6

January 1
Ephesians 5:14 Awaken thou that sleepest, Christ has arisen. Today will begin your new day in Christ Jesus to come alive, take a deep breath, relax, and don't look back on your past mistakes - they are over. Awaken to become all that God has planned for you today.

January 2
James 1:2-4 Consider it pure joy, my brothers, whenever you face trials of many kinds, because you know that the testing of your faith develops perseverance. God presents trials to us so that we can develop perseverance and our faith may be mature and complete, not lacking in anything. Give God praise today and every day, and remember that our tests are His way of preparing us for His Kingdom's work

January 3
Romans 10:17 Faith comes by hearing and hearing by the Word of God. The Lord is speaking to you today, come closer to His face so you can hear what He is saying. Open up your spiritual ears and heart to listen and obey your Heavenly Father. Today is the day to get quiet and listen to your orders from Heaven - what to do and where to go. You have all the faith you need to hear and obey your Heavenly Father.

January 4
Philippians 4:13 I can do all things through Christ that strengthens me. Today, with Jesus on your side, you are given a Supernatural Strength to go forward and triumph over whatever lies ahead. The Way Maker has already made the way straight. Go forth in peace.

January 5
Luke 12:48 To whom much is given much will be required. Let us begin this day with a shout of praise unto the Lord. The Lord gave so much for us when He died on the cross- our lives should be totally devoted to Him.

January 6
Proverbs 2:6 The Lord gives wisdom; from His mouth comes knowledge and understanding. Early we shall rise and ask for wisdom to make Godly decisions that will change the world in which we live. Today I will seek the Lord's face for truth. This is the day that the Lord has made.

January 7
Isaiah 26:3 You will keep in perfect peace him whose mind is steadfast, because he trusts in You. You must speak the Word of God; hold on, this too shall come to pass. Victory is yours today.

January 8
Psalms 27:1 The Lord is my light and my salvation, whom shall I fear? The Lord is the stronghold of my life- of whom shall I be afraid? Fear not for the Lord thy God is with you today and forever. Hold your head up, look towards the Hill from which cometh all your help, fear not about your tomorrow.

January 9
Psalm 126:6 He that goeth forth and weepeth, bearing precious seed, shall doubtless come again with rejoicing, bringing his sheaves with him. It's ok to cry, you are sowing seeds into the earth, and your harvest will come forth in God's timing. Wait on the Lord with much joy in your heart.

January 10
James 4:10 Humble yourselves in the sight of the Lord, and he shall lift you up. Today allow the Lord to humble you to love others more. Share with others how the Lord is transforming you into His image for His Kingdom's use.

January 11
Proverbs 19:23 The fear of the Lord tendeth to life, and he that hath it shall abide satisfied. Fear nothing but the Lord. Fear not man or your tomorrows.

January 12
Psalm 32:8 I will instruct thee and teach thee in the way which thou shalt go: I will guide thee with mine eye. Let go and allow God to teach you all things. He is the only One that has traveled the path that will come your way. Enjoy communion with Him.

January 13
Psalm 50:15 Call upon me in the day of trouble, I will deliver thee, and thou shalt glorify me. Today is your time to call on the Lord, He waits this special time to speak to you, come unto me, I will answer all that concern you.

January 14
Matthew 11:28 Come unto me, all ye that labor and are heavy laden, and I will give you rest. Our God will comfort your soul today. Rest, Relax and Restore your mind. Allow the Holy Spirit to bring calmness to your whole being.

January 15
Luke 21:33 Heaven and earth shall pass away, but my Word shall not pass away. God's Word is true and his Word shall come to pass. Read His Word day & night.

January 16
John 6:35 I am the bread of life, he that cometh to me shall never hunger; and he that believeth on me shall never thirst. You're thirsty season is over!

January 17
Psalm 84:11 The Lord will give grace and glory: no good thing will He withhold from them that walk uprightly. Walk not after the flesh, but learn how to walk Holy. The Holy Spirit will teach you all things, call on Him, He will answer today.

January 18
John 10:9 I am the door: by me if any man enters in, he shall be saved, and shall go in and out, and find pasture. I will seek the door today; I shall go forth in my faith.

January 19
Jeremiah 29: 11 I know the Plans, I have for you declares the Lord, plans to prosper you and not harm you, plans to give you hope and a future. I made you in my own image; allow me to reveal all the wonderful plans I have for your future.

January 20
Psalm 68:19 Blessed be the Lord, who daily loadeth us with benefits. I will bless you today with some new benefits from above, because I love you so much. I await you.

January 21
John 14; 19 Yet a little while and the world seeth me no more; but ye see me; because I live, ye shall live also. You can live through me; I am He that died for you.

January 22
2Corinthians 12:9 My grace is sufficient for thee: for my strength is made perfect in weakness. You may feel weak, but I am always here to give you strength in your weakness. Today you are right where I need you to be; to show myself strong.

January 23
Matthew 21:22 All things, whatsoever ye shall ask in prayer, believing, ye shall receive. Help me, dear Father, to believe that you will provide for me this day.

January 24
Matthew 5:10 Blessed are they which are persecuted for righteousness sake: for theirs is the Kingdom of Heaven. You must endure this hardship only for a season.

January 25
John 14:14 If ye shall ask anything in my name, I will do it. Lord thank you for the availability of your Spirit to sustain me during my testing times.

January 26
1Peter 3:12 For the eyes of the Lord are over the righteous and his ears are open unto their prayers. The Lord will answer all your prayers in His timing. Yes it is so!

January 27
Psalm 86:7 In the day of my trouble I will call upon thee: for thou will answer me. Today, expect an answer to your prayers. You will receive the breakthrough you have been waiting for!

January 28
Exodus 15:2 The Lord is my strength and song, and he is my salvation. Your strength will come only from the Lord.

January 29
Genesis 9:11 *I will establish my covenant with you: neither shall there anymore be a flood to destroy the earth.* God has a covenant to make with you, your flood days are over on this earth. Praise Him just because of who He is. Love has no sorrow.

January 30
Matthew 24:13 He that shall endure unto the end, the same shall be saved. You have all that you need to endure, look with-in its right there, you belong to the Lord

January 31
2 Corinthians 5:17 *Therefore if any man be in Christ, he is a new creature: old things are passed away; behold all things are become new.* Lord, thank you for making me a new creature, cleanse my soul of old things. I accept, I am new…

My Testimony: *My life is so blessed to be chosen to complete my first book 2009. The journey has change my life, taught me to pray more, I been given a new praise how to keep stepping with an unspeakable joy, over all the stepping stones that came my way. I have learned to wait on the Lord Jesus to teach me whatever I need to know to complete the Vision that He given me to finish. Always remember what God gave you, He will hold you accountable for the dream and vision to come forth as the Visionary. Praise God, He will get the Glory from my life!!!*

"When We are Weak, He is Strong With-in Us"

By: Co-Pastor, Prophetess,
Meliza Woodward

February
Walking By Faith, Not by Sight
2 Corinthians 5:7

February 1
John 14:27 *Peace I leave with you, my peace I give unto you... let not your heart be troubled, neither let it be afraid.* Fear not, for God is with you. Hold on to your Peace.

February 2
Ephesians 5:14 *Awake thou that sleepest, and arise from the dead, and Christ shall give thee light.* Disregard who the enemy says you are! Christ desires that you know Him for who He is- He is everything you need to step out of darkness and into light.

February 3
Revelation 3:12 *Him that overcometh will I make a pillar in the temple of my God.* The Lord chose you as a pillar in His temple to uphold His Glory.

February 4
Galatians 4:19 *My dear children, for whom I am, again in the pains of childbirth until Christ is formed in you.* Take a deep breath, this time in your life is only to birth your gifts into the earth, not unto death.

February 5
Psalm 119:11 *Your Word, I have hidden in my heart that I might not sin against you.* Lord, help me to always keep your Word in my heart.

February 6
Daniel 6:27 *He delivers and rescues and He works signs and wonders in Heaven and on earth.* Reveal more to me, O Lord, of your works, may it be unto me.

February 7
John 16:13 *Allow the Spirit of Truth to come, He will guide you into all truths.* May today be your day to know the truth about who you really are.

February 8
Jeremiah 33:6 *Today I will heal them and reveal to them the abundance of peace and truth.* Peace is all around you and your family. Open up your mouth and command peace to come forth in Jesus' name.

February 9
Psalm 103:14 *He knows our frame; He remembers that we are dust.* Enjoy this day in the sunshine, walking on the dirt from which we came.

February 10
John 15:5 *Without Me, you are nothing.* Always keep the Lord thy God before anything and anyone.

February 11
John 10:10 *I have come that they may have life and that they may have it more abundantly. Today is your day to have all that God has for you.*

February 12
Romans 12:17 *Never pay back evil for evil to anyone. Respect what is right in the sight of all men.* Overcome evil with good. Do something good for those who do evil deeds towards you.

February 13
Acts 10:34-35 *Opening his mouth, Peter said: "I most certainly understand now that God is not one to show partiality, but in every nation the man who fears Him and does what is right is welcome to Him."* God shows no partiality; whoever fears Him and works righteously will be rewarded.

February 14
Ephesians 4:32 *Be kind to one another, tender hearted and forgiving, just as God has forgiven you.* Pray for and forgive those who have hurt or caused offense towards you.

February 15
Philippians 1:9 *I pray that your love may abound still more and more in knowledge and all discernment in others.* Learn to love through the pains & hurts.

February 16
Psalm 24:1 *The earth is the Lord's and all its fullness, the world and those who dwell therein.* You belong to the Lord and you are an example of the Lord's beauty in the earth.

February 17
Psalm 20:2 *May He send you help from the sanctuary and grant you support from Zion.* Help is given to you today: open your heart and receive it!

February 18
Psalm 23:3 *He restores my soul, He guides me in paths of righteousness for His name's sake.* You are restored in your soul, and will be guided by the Almighty hand of the Lord.

February 19
Psalm 27:1 *The Lord is my light and my salvation, whom shall I fear?* Cast away all fears today. Let the light of the Lord shine upon your path so you can see the way.

February 20
Proverbs 14:26 *In the fear of the Lord there is strong confidence, and His children will have a place of refuge.* To fear the Lord is the beginning of wisdom.

February 21
Lamentations 3:26 *It is good that one should hope and wait quietly for the Salvation of the Lord.*

February 22
Ephesians 5:8,10 *....Walk as children of light... finding out what is acceptable to the Lord.* Let your light shine before all men.

February 23
Luke 12:48 *....To whom much is given much will be required.....You can do all things that the Lord will require of you in these last days, with His help.*

February 24
Psalm 85:7 *Show us your unfailing love, O Lord, and grant us your salvation.* Reveal more of your Love my God, so I can share with others.

February 25
1 Corinthians 1:9 *God is faithful, by whom you were called into fellowship of His Son, Jesus Christ our Lord.* *If you stay faithful to a faithful God, all your dreams will come true.*

February 26
Matthew 10:30 *The very hairs of your head are all numbered.* You do matter to the Lord, and are precious in His sight.

February 27
Romans 10:17 **Faith** *comes by hearing and hearing by the Word of God.* Pray and let the Lord lead you to a church home, where you can learn God's Word and grow.

February 28
2 Corinthians 6:16 *....I will dwell in them, and walk among them, I will be their God, and they shall be my people.* *You are chosen to do Great things for the Kingdom of God in this hour...*

February 29
Psalm 85:13 *Righteousness goes before him and prepares the way for his steps.* Always pray for the Lord to order your steps.

Testimony:

I am so Thankful to the Lord for allowing me to get a full Track Scholarship, that paid my way through College. My mother Meliza taught me to pray about everything, not only pray, but believe by faith what you ask the Lord shall come to pass. I just wanted to give hope to single mother, keep praying, teach your children to pray for the father's that are not there, to keep them lifted up anyhow, this is how your blessings will come back into your children. My mother taught me how to love, pray, believe the impossible dreams. I am now a Wife, Mother, and a Teacher of the Arts in Theater, all because I was taught to pray and not hate those who was not there to support my dreams. " Keep Dreaming " Dreams do come True....

"We Shall Walk into Our Destiny by Faith"

By: Co-Owner, Director, Producer, Actress,
Tarjatta Rose- Johnson

March
"Jesus Christ is the True Vine, We are the Branches"
John 15:1-27

March 1
John 19:11 *Jesus answered, "You would have no power over me if it were not given to you from above. Therefore the one who handed me over to you is guilty of a greater sin."* The Lord will lighten your darkness. You are no longer in that dark place - it was just a place of testing. You have passed all that was required of you.

March 2
Matthew 18:22 *Jesus answered, "I tell you, not seven times, but seventy-seven times."* You're forgiven seventy times seven, Jesus Christ says so. All your sins are behind you. I have forgotten all that you have done, says the Lord.

March 3
Psalm 31:24 *Be of good courage, and He shall strengthen your heart, all ye that hope in the Lord.* Today, I am here to encourage you to keep going on. God is all the strength you need.

March 4
2 Samuel 22:7 *In my distress I called to the Lord; I called out to my God. From His temple He heard my voice; my cry came to His ears.* Call upon the Lord in your distress for He will hear and answer. He is the answer to all that you have asked, it is done today. He has moved the things that have kept you bound. Say today, all is well with my soul.

March 5
Galatians 1:3 *Grace and peace to you from God the Father and from our Lord Jesus Christ.* Receive the peace that the Lord gives to you. No man can give you what He gives freely.

March 6
Galatians 1:15 *But when it pleased God who separated me from my mother's womb and called me by His Grace...* His grace is with you today and is forever with thee. His grace kept you when you wanted to let go. He was right there.

March 7
Galatians 1:16 ...*God revealed His Son in me and I conferred not with flesh and blood.* The Lord Jesus Christ the anointed one, who died because He loves you. He sits at the Father's right side praying for you.

March 8
Romans 8:28 *And, all things work together for good to them that love God, to them who are called according to His purpose.* Everything you have endured is for His Glory.

March 9
Isaiah 43:1 *.....For I have redeemed thee, I have called thee by thy name; thou art mine.* He is the one who has redeemed the time, now it's your time to be brought forth into the earth for all men to see that you belong to me.

March 10
Isaiah 43:10 *Ye are my witness saith the Lord.....*Arise and stand for God as He stands in you. You are chosen by God.

March 11
Psalm 91:1 *He that dwelleth in the secret place of the Most High shall abide under the shadow of the Almighty.* Your time has arrived, come forth like the mighty warrior that you are. Now!

March 12
1 Corinthians 12:27 *Now ye are the body of Christ and members in particular.* We are one, just as the Father and Son are one.

March 13
1Corinthians 12:13 *For by one Spirit are we all baptized into one body. Whether we be Jews or Gentiles, whether we be bond or free; and have been all made to drink into one Spirit.* Drink from the fountain of living water; refresh yourself today with the water that He gives to you.

March 14
1 Corinthians 12:14 *For the body is not one member but many.* God loves you, and created you for such a time like this.

March 15
Matthew 16:19 *And I will give unto thee the keys of the Kingdom of Heaven….*I give the keys of heaven to you; no weapon formed against you shall overcome who you are in me.

March 16
Matthew 16:18 *Upon this Rock I will build my Church and the gates of hell shall not prevail against it.* Today you must open up your mouth and declare "I will NOT be moved."

March 17
Matthew 16:19 *....And, whatever thou shalt bind on earth shall be bound in Heaven.* Speak the Lord's Words openly for all men to hear and see His power.

March 18
1Corinthians 13:1 *Though I speak with the tongues of men and of angels, and have not charity, I am become as sounding brass or a tinkling cymbal.* You are His servant; speak to His people, and ready them for His return.

March 19
John 10:14 *I am the good shepherd; I know my sheep and my sheep know me.* Jesus Christ is the Good Shepherd; He knows you. He is well pleased with you, His faithful servant.

March 20
John 10:29 *My Father, who has given them to me, is greater than all; no one can snatch them out of my Father's hand.* No one can pluck you out of God's hand. Whatever the Father giveth to the Son, no man or devil can take away.

March 21
John 10:27 *My sheep hear my voice, and I know them, and they follow me.* Keep your ears in tune with the time you are in; He will order your very steps.

March 22
1 Peter 3:10 *For he that will love life, and see good days, let him refrain his tongue from evil, and his lips that they speak no guile.* Speak only things that you hear God say, no longer what you want to say to His people.

March 23
1 Peter 3:12 *For the eyes of the Lord are over the righteous, and his ears are open unto their prayers: but the face of the Lord is against them that do evil.* God's eyes are upon His servants, your rewards will be great.

March 24
1 Peter 3;14 *But, if ye suffer for righteousness sake happy are ye: and be not afraid of their terror, neither be troubled.* Your suffering is not in vain. I see and I know all that you have done for the Kingdom.

March 25
1 Peter 13:15 *But, sanctify the Lord God in your hearts....* You know God as the greater one who is within. Never forget to whom you belong; He is your God until the end of time.

March 26
Hebrews 13:5 *....I will never leave thee nor forsake thee.* God is with you always. All your tests and trials shall pass in His timing, not your timing. Trust Him concerning this time in your life.

March 27
Hebrews 13:6 *The Lord is my helper and I will not fear what man shall do unto me.* Fear not, this is only a test, you shall pass.... His Words shall never return unto me void, it shall do only what He has spoken.

March 28
Jeremiah 29:11 *The Lord says He knows the thoughts He has towards you; they're of peace and not evil, to give you an expected end.* His plans are great concerning your future; lean not to your ways, but let Him lead the way, it is the right way.

March 29
Matthew 24:13 *But he that endure unto the end the same shall be saved.* You have endured much, and He will reward you openly so that all can see how good He is to those whom He loves.

March 30
Isaiah 54:5 *For thy maker is thine husband; the Lord of host is His name….The God of the whole earth shall He be called.* He is all that you will ever need; He is wiping all the tears from your face. Press close to Him and feel His hand.

March 31
Revelation 2:7 *He that hath an ear, let him hear what the Spirit saith unto the Churches. To him that overcometh will I give to eat of the tree of life, which is in the midst of the paradise of God.* Today come and sup with Him. The table is set for those who have overcome the troubles of this world. Rest today in paradise with God.

My Testimony:

The Lord healed me and delivered me from the use of drugs, set me free from an abusive husband who was also unfaithful. There so much more that the Lord has done and is doing in my life. I've surrendered my will to God to do His will in the earth. I am an Ordained Minister, I'm a servant, friend and a daughter of the most High God through Jesus Christ my Lord and Savior.

Prophetess Sharon Bacchus

April
Month of God's Refreshing

April 1
Psalm 94:17 *Unless the Lord has given me help, I would soon have dwelt in the silence of death.* Allow God to be your help today.

April 2
Psalm 142:8 *Then the righteous will gather about me because of your goodness to me.* Declare "I will see the goodness of God in the land of the living!"

April 3
Hosea 6:3 *Let us acknowledge the Lord; let us press on to acknowledge Him. As surely as the sun rises, he will appear, he will come to us like the winter rains, like the spring rains that water the earth.* God is with you – His spirit refreshes the weary.

April 4
Isaiah 49:16 *See I have engraved you on the palms of my hands; your walls are ever before me.* Meditate on the love of God. You are in His heart.

April 5
Jeremiah 31:14 *I will satisfy the priests with abundance and my people will be filled with my bounty declares the Lord.* His provision will overtake your life. Ask in faith and you shall receive.

April 6
Job 36:15 But those who suffer he delivers from their suffering; he speaks to them in their affliction. Say a prayer today for someone you know who is hurting. He will comfort you in your time of need.

April 7
Psalm 42:8 By day the Lord directs his love, at night his song is with me – a prayer to the God of my life. Sing a new song unto the Lord – His love is unfailing.

April 8
Isaiah 2:22 Stop trusting in man who has but a breath in his nostrils. Of what account is he? Put your trust today in the One who cannot disappoint.

April 9
Isaiah 32:17 *The fruit of righteousness will be peace; the effect of righteousness will be quietness and confidence forever.* Allow the peace of God to rule in your heart - extend His peace to your family.

April 10
Isaiah 35:4 Be strong, do not fear, Your God will come, he will come with vengeance; with divine retribution he will come to save you. Don't take justice into your own hands. Allow God to save and deliver you from all your enemies.

April 11
Isaiah 61:9 Their descendants will be known among the nations & their offspring among the peoples. All who see them will acknowledge that they are a people the Lord has blessed.
Pray for the children in your life. God's hand of blessing will cover them.

April 12
John 6:44 *No one can come to me unless the Father who sent me draws him, and I will raise him up at that day.* Pray for the Lord to draw a lost soul you know to the Light of His Love.

April 13
John 10:4 *When he has brought out all his own, he goes on ahead of them and his sheep follow him because they know his voice.* He is your Shepherd – follow His leading today.

April 14
Luke 1:38 I am the Lord's servant, Mary answered. May it be to me as you have said. Then the angel left her. Yield to the will of God – You won't regret it.

April 15
*Daniel 4:3 How great are his signs how mightily his wonders! His kingdom is an eternal kingdom; his dominion endures from generation to generation .*Live in light of eternity.

April 16
Deuteronomy 30:15 See I set before you today life and prosperity, death and destruction. Make choices which glorify God.

April 17
Ephesians 6:10-12 Finally, be strong in the Lord and in his mighty power. Put on the full armor of God so that you can take your stand against the devil's schemes. For our struggle is not against flesh and blood, but against the rulers, against the authorities, against the powers of this dark world and against the spiritual forces of evil in the heavenly realms. Recognize the work of the enemy and put on your armor today!

April 18
Ephesians 4:31-32 Get rid of all bitterness, rage, anger, harsh words, and slander, as well as all types of evil behavior. Instead, be kind to each other, tenderhearted, forgiving one another, just

as God through Christ has forgiven you. A heart of forgiveness is one which is tender towards God. Release others daily.

April 19
Colossians 1:11 ...being strengthened with all power according to his glorious might so that you may have great endurance and patience, and joyfully. The Lord has equipped you with endurance and patience to finish your race victoriously!

April 20
Proverbs 25:15 Through patience a ruler can be persuaded, and a gentle tongue can break a bone. Use the power of gentle words to win others to Christ.

April 21
Ecclesiastes 7:8 The end of a matter is better than its beginning, and patience is better than pride. Look for opportunities today to demonstrate the fruit of patience.

April 22
Mark 10:1 People were bringing little children to Jesus to have him touch them, but the disciples rebuked them. Ask God today to give you wisdom and discernment when dealing with the children in your life. Allow them to become as precious to you as they are to Him.

April 23
Psalm 17:6 I call on you, O God, for you will answer me; give ear to me and hear my prayer. God hears the faintest cries of our hearts. Put down the telephone and call out to Him.

April 24
Psalm 66:16 Come and listen, all you who fear God; let me tell you what he has done for me. Expect fresh testimonies and miracles! Share with others the great things God has done in your life.

April 25
Matthew 25:21 His master replied, "Well done, good and faithful servant! You have been faithful with a few things; I will put you in charge of many things. Come and share your master's happiness!" Imitate the faithfulness of God. Show Him today you can be trusted with more. Ask Him to show you practical ways to balance your priorities.

April 26
Ephesians 6:7 Serve wholeheartedly, as if you were serving the Lord, not men... Make a commitment to ask God to show you how to serve Him wholeheartedly in all that you do.

April 27
Jeremiah 5:24 It never occurs to them to say, "How can we honor our God with our lives, The God who gives rain in both spring and autumn and maintains the rhythm of the seasons." What

does it mean to honor God with your life? Use your life to refresh others.

April 28
Matthew 10:42 And if anyone gives even a cup of cold water to one of these little ones because he is my disciple, I tell you the truth, he will certainly not lose his reward. Let others experience Christ through you.

April 29
Philippians 3:8 What is more, I consider everything a loss compared to the surpassing greatness of knowing Christ Jesus my Lord, for whose sake I have lost all things. I consider them rubbish that I may gain Christ. Think today about a time when you have clearly seen Jesus. Thank him for being a God who is near.

April 30
Matthew 5:8 Blessed are the pure in heart, for they will see God. Pray this prayer: "Lord, help me to hear Your voice. Allow my heart to get quiet long enough to sit and listen to your encouragement and instructions. Give me the courage Lord to obey you. Amen."

My Testimony:

Before I was born again as most young adults I enjoyed partying with friends, drinking, sex out of wedlock, cursing and just living life with nothing on my mind but ME. When I turned 23 years old, I noticed a shift in my life and I didn't really understand what was happening.

I gradually lost my desire to drink, hang out with wild friends and have illicit sexual relationships. I didn't know Jesus but was miraculously "delivered" from many carnal desires, I believe because of the prayers of my mother, aunts and grandmother. I felt a void, an emptiness in my life and started to read the Bible and watch Christian television.

Much of the Bible didn't make sense to me although I longed to find the answers to my empty, purposeless life. One night, my aunt invited me to attend a revival. I thought, oh well, I don't have anything else to do since I'd dropped contact with my "party buddies" so I went.

That night, as the evangelist preached I listen and felt the nudge of God. Although I had heard many calls to salvation, actually every Sat or Sun for most of my life, this time things were different. The Holy Spirit knew I was ready. That night in my seat in a sea full of people I quietly prayed the sinners pray and accepted Jesus as my Lord and Savior.

I didn't respond go to the altar but in my heart I knew a change was taking place. My burdens were lifted and I felt I had connected to something, someone more powerful than anything I've ever experienced.

I eventually answered an altar call, was baptized and became an active member of a local church but my testimony is what salvation is all about. It's a personal relationship with Jesus. It's a heart to heart connection with our Savior.

He doesn't always deliver us from our strongholds before He saves us as He did with me, but it reminds me of His great love for humanity. Our God is a BIG God. We can't put Him in a box.

He does what He wants and how He wants. I'm so glad that He thought enough to change my hard heart to one of flesh. Now I am filled with purpose, peace and most importantly His LOVE.

"God's Word is True"

Prophetess, Unisha Marshall

May
"Completely Surrender"

May 1
Proverbs 3:5: Trust in the Lord with all your heart and lean not on your own understanding. According to God's word, when we trust in Him and commit to doing His will, He will lead us to the Promised Land.

May 2
Exodus 15:6 Your right hand, O LORD, was majestic in power. Your right hand, O LORD, shattered the enemy. I am the same God that parted the Red Sea for my children, single-handedly delivering them from the hands of the enemy.

I AM the same God that can deliver you my child from your enemies, if you will surrender them to me. I know how to fight your battle the right way.

May 3
Psalm 91:1 He who dwells in the shelter of the Most High will rest in the shadow of the Almighty. You will find safety in His Word - it is a Living Word; it is what keeps you. It was given to us to guide, teach and heal. The Word is our hiding place.

May 4
1 Chronicles 28:9 If you seek him, he will be found by you. The Lord waits for us to come to Him, He want us to give Him our yoke and burdens in exchange for His. Did He not say that His yoke is easy and His burden is light? He waits and waits for us to finally, realize that the burdens we carry are too heavy.

May 5
Psalm 27:1 The LORD is my light and my salvation; whom shall I fear? The Lord knows where we are to travel, even though we may get lost at times. He has thoughts and plans for us; we should just let Him be our guide, and trust Him to see us through.

May 6
Isaiah 43: 18-19 Forget the former things; do not dwell on the past. See, I am doing a new thing! Now it springs up; do you not perceive it? I am making a way in the desert and streams in the

wasteland. The Lord is saying:"Here my child, let go: you are holding on to things that are keeping you from being free. You can move on if you surrender everything that is negative. Look and see: I am trying to move you into your season of harvest, but you have to move forward by letting go of all the negative yesterdays.

May 7
Ephesians 6:10 Finally, be strong in the Lord and in His mighty power. Through Paul the Lord is saying: Let me do the impossible, the branch cannot do things in themselves - they need the vine to see them through.

May 8
2 Timothy: 2:3 Endure hardship with us like a good soldier of Christ Jesus. Don't faint, don't surrender. The Lord is your strength, He will see you through.

May 9
James 2: 14-17 What good is it, my brothers, if a man claims to have faith but has no deeds? Can such faith save him? Suppose a brother or sister is without clothes and daily food. If one of you says to him, "Go, I wish you well; keep warm and well fed," but does nothing about his physical needs, what good is it? In the same way, faith by itself, if it is not accompanied by action, is dead. What good is it to have a faith and not use it to change the lives of those around us?

Why have faith and not use it to change the world? A faith that does not have action to back it up is no faith at all.

May 10
Psalm 119:89-90 Forever, O Lord, your word is settled in heaven. Your faithfulness continues throughout all generations; You established the earth, and it stands. Today is a new day in your life to let go of what you want. Trust God's spoken word to establish your next step with Him.

May 11
1 Peter 1: 13-16 Therefore, prepare your minds for action; be self-controlled; set your hope fully on the grace to be given you when Jesus Christ is revealed. As obedient children, do not conform to the evil desires you had when you lived in ignorance. But just as he who called you is holy, so be holy in all you do; for it is written: Be holy, because I am holy. We have been given new life in Christ! We must align our hopes and minds with His, and we cannot allow ourselves to slip back into the sin that once controlled our lives. We must strive to be holy, just as our Creator is holy.

May 12
Romans 8:14 For, as many as are led by the Spirit of God, these are Sons of God. When you are led by the Spirit of God, you are in His will, because it is none of you and all of Him. He has all of you!

May 13
Mark 10:15 Anyone who refuses to come to God as a little child will never be allowed into His Kingdom. Little children are so open. Be like that child and allow God to work through and in you. The Lord will not withhold any good thing from His child.

May 14
Isaiah 29:19 The humble also shall increase their joy in the Lord. Total surrender will bring you nothing but joy from the Lord.

May15
Psalm 25:4 Show me your ways, O Lord; teach me your paths. The Lord is excited to do just that, because He created us for Himself.

May 16
Revelation 2:7 To Him who overcomes, I will give to eat from the tree of life. If we do not give up on ourselves and on what God has for us, He will reward us with the gifts He promised to Adam and Eve, the same gifts He will give us at the end of this world.

May 17
Psalm 18:32 It is God who arms me with strength, and makes my way perfect. The Lord knows what is ahead, so He knows what it will take to prepare you to fight the battle.

May 18
Proverbs 3:6 In all your ways acknowledge Him and He shall direct your paths. He knows where you need to go, and what you need to get you there. Let Him show you the way.

May 19
Romans 5:1 Having been justified by faith, we have peace with God through our Lord Jesus Christ. What Jesus has done for us is the reason why we have to seek him.

May 20
1Peter 1:8 Though now you do not see Him, yet believing, you join with joy inexpressible and full of glory.

May 21
1 John 5:14 "This is the confidence that we have in life, that if we ask anything according to His will, He hears us." God hears our prayers. If our prayers align with His will, we can rest assured, knowing that He will fulfill them.

May 22
Hosea 2:15 I will give back her vineyards to her and transform her Valley of Troubles into a door of hope. He is going to restore what was taken from you. Hold on, He will give you more than you lost.

May 23
John 16:13 When He, the Spirit of Truth, has come, He will bring you into all Truths. The Holy Spirit knows what the Father and Son want for us, and He knows how to get us there.

May 24
Galatians 5:22-23 The fruit of the Spirit is Love, Joy, Peace, Longsuffering, Kindness, Goodness, Faithfulness, Gentleness, and Self-Control. Be filled today with New Fruits of the Spirit, today is your day to receive a free gift from the Lord.

May 25
Joel 2:25-26 I will restore to you the years that the swarming locusts have eaten…. You shall … praise the name of the Lord your God. This is your season; do not jump ship.

May 26
1 Corinthians 1:25 The foolishness of God is wiser than men, and the weakness of God is stronger than men. We are only humans, created in the image of an all-mighty God. He is wise and He is strong, and even at His worst, He is still all-powerful.

May 27
Proverbs 22:6 Train up a child in the way he should go, and when he is old he will not depart from it. What is planted cannot be uprooted if it is planted according to God's Word.

May 28
Proverbs 16:20 He who heeds the Word wisely will find good and whoever trusts in the Lord, happy is he. The Word is God's blueprint and He is your anchor.

May 29
Psalm 115:1 Not unto us, O Lord, not unto us, but to Your name give Glory. It is not about us, it is all about the Lord. He deserves the Glory and rightfully so. Without Him, we can do nothing.

May 30
Lamentations 3:26 It is good that one should hope and wait quietly for the salvation of the Lord. When we are still and wait faithfully on the Lord, we receive His blessings and salvation.

May 31
Proverbs 2:6 The Lord gives wisdom; from His mouth comes knowledge and understanding. When we ask for wisdom, the Lord will give it to us freely. He is the ultimate source of knowledge and wisdom.

My Testimony:

The Lord brought to my mind, tonight, what another prophetess said to me a year ago she saw me writing a book. The thought came to my head at that time, me Lord write a book, I knew it was God speaking through her, but I did not see myself being a writer, I would think about it, actually the thought came to my mine, when I was at Family Christian bookstore, looking at their rack of small inspirational books, and thinking, maybe I am to write a small book like these. And now and after all of that, I now know that it was calendar, book with other women. With God using you Prophetess Meliza. Just remember when God speaks to His child, that He is going to do something. He is faithful to bring all things to pass that was spoken,

Love you

Song73S@peoplepc.com

By: Apostle, Ann St. Bernard

June

"Becoming a Warrior for the Kingdom of God"
Ephesians 6:10-17

June 1
John 14:27 Peace I leave with you, my peace I give unto you, let not your heart be troubled, neither let it be afraid. Fear not, I am with you. Hold on to your peace.

June 2
Ephesians 5:14 Awake thou that sleepest, and arise from the dead and Christ shall give thee light. Shrug off your sleep- open your eyes to Christ and see the hope He has for you!

June 3
Revelation 3:12 Him that overcometh will I make a pillar in the temple of my God. The Lord chose you as His pillar in His temple, to uphold His Glory.

June 4
Galatians 4:19 My dear children, for whom I am, again in the pains of childbirth until Christ is formed in you. Take a deep breath and know that this time in your life is only to birth your gifts into the earth.

June 5
John 14:1 Let not your Heart be troubled. Trust God to bring you through this trying time; He will work it out.

June 6
Proverbs 22:17 Incline your ears and hear the words of the wise, and apply your heart to my knowledge. Listen to the voice of the Lord.

June 7
1Peter 1:8 Though, now you don't see Him, yet believing, you rejoice with Joy. Today, let me lead you by my Spirit. I am the Spirit of truth. Rejoice and expect the many blessings that are on the way.

June 8
Habakkuk 2:3 For the vision is yet for an appointed time; but at the end it will speak and it will not lie. Though it tarries, wait for it, because it will surely come, it will not tarry. Wait upon the Lord. Write down your vision; it shall come forth in the name of Jesus.

June 9
1 John 4:7 Beloved, let us love one another, for love is of God. Today is your day to pour out love upon your enemy; you will be blessed for showing love.

June 10
Mark 11:24 So I tell you, whatever you pray for and ask, believe that you have got it and you shall have it. May your prayers storm the Heavens. Pray today and ask for something special, it shall be given unto you by your faith. Amen.

June 11
Ezra 8:21 The hand of our God is upon all those who seek Him for the good of mankind. Bow humbly before God. His hand will be upon you to lift you up again.

June 12
Psalm 46:1 God is our refuge and strength, a very present help in time of trouble. I stretch my hands towards thee today O Lord to help me overcome my fleshly weakness. I will lean on the Lord in these trying times. I've got the Victory in Jesus!

June 13
Psalm 71:1 In you, O Lord, I put my trust; let me never be put to shame. I command shame to lose me, to set me free in the name of Jesus. No longer will shame keep me bound. I am free to tell my story without shame and may my past help someone else.

June 14
Colossians 3:23 Whatever you do, do it heartily, as to the Lord and not to men. Today, I will do my works unto thee, no longer trying to please men.

June 15
Hebrews 13:5 I will never leave you nor forsake you. Come to a quiet place with me; close your eyes - I am with thee wherever you go.

June 16
Psalm 61:1-3 Hear my cry, O God attend to my prayer. From the end of the earth. I will cry to you, lead me to the rock that is higher than I. For you have been a shelter for me. Trust in the shelter of His wings. When everyone hurts you and leaves you, the Lord will be there to pick you up. When one door is closed God will open a new door that no man can shut.

June 17
Psalm 23:1-3 The Lord is my shepherd. I shall not want. He makes me to lie down in green pastures; He leads me beside the still waters. He restores my soul. Amid the pain and life's ups and downs, God is so good. He will ALWAYS be there when you need Him.

June 18
Jeremiah 31:3 The Lord has appeared to me saying; yes I have loved you with an everlasting love; therefore with loving kindness, I have drawn you again, I will build you and you shall be rebuilt and shall go forth in the dances of those who rejoice. Today, get up and dance unto the Lord!

June 19
Luke11:9-10 So, I say to you: Ask, and it will be given to you; seek, and you will find; knock and it will be opened to you. For everyone who asks receives; and he who seeks finds. Go forth and fulfill the vision that God has given you. It's your time.

June 20
2 Corinthians 8:16 But thanks be to God who puts the same earnest care for you, into the heart of Titus. For he not only accepted exhortation, but comes to you of his own accord. Come today with thanksgiving in your heart, receive the promises from God for you and your family.

June 21
Romans 12:2 And, do not be conformed to this World, but be transformed by the renewing of your mind, that you may prove what is that good and acceptable and perfect will of God. Start your day off with good thinking, remember this is a new day!

June 22
Psalm 100:4-5 Be, thankful to Him, and bless his name. For the Lord is good; His mercy is everlasting and His truth endures to all generations. You are covered under God's mercy today and forever.

June 23
Proverbs 8:33-36 Hear instruction and be wise, and do not disdain it, blessed is the man who listen to me. He, who sins against me, wrongs his own soul. Ask your Heavenly Father for wisdom; it is yours when you ask in faith.

June 24
John 16:22 Therefore you now have sorrow: but I will see you again and your heart will rejoice, and your joy on one will take from you. Whatever you ask the Father in my name He will give you.

June 25
Proverbs 13:26 The righteous should choose his friends carefully, for the way of the wicked leads them astray. Allow the Lord to send the friends He has for you, they will love you unconditional.

June 26
Isaiah 66:1 Heaven is my throne and earth is my footstool. Where is the house that you will build me? Relax, the Lord already has a beautiful home just for you, in His timing you will receive.

June 27
Matthew 5:44 But I say to you, love your enemies, bless those who curse you, do good to those who hate you, and pray for those who spitefully use you and persecute you. Bow down and pray for all those who have hurt you, forgive them today and get free from the bondages that had you hostage so long. Today is you day of Change!

June 28
Matthew 12:18 Behold! My servant whom I have chosen, my beloved in whom my soul is well pleased! Rejoice, forever are the beloved and chosen servants of the Lord!

June 29
John 3:16 For God so loved the world that He gave His only begotten Son, that whoever believes in him should not perish, but have everlasting life. You are that Special to God, just Believe.....

June 30
1Corinthians 1:3 Grace to you and peace from God our Father and the Lord Jesus Christ. Your Heavenly Father will bless you with all the comforts and joys because He cares for you.

My Testimony:
The Lord is so good in my life, I have had many struggles in life, with the help of the Lord I have overcame them all. Sometimes in life you will want to give-up, but you can't because Jesus died just for you and me to be who we are today. A word of encouragement keep the Faith, "God is able" to do exceedingly more than what you see today, you will be greater in the fullness of God's timing.

"GOD IS ABLE"

By: Psalmist, Tanya Woodward-Hadley

JULY
"Joy of the Lord is your Strength"

July 1
Galatians 5:25 If we live in the Spirit let us also walk in the Spirit. Go take a nice walk in the fresh air, let go and let God have this day. Peace is yours this day!

July 2
Psalm 31:19 How great is your goodness, which you have laid up for those who fear you. Stop looking at what appears to be; keep your eyes on the goodness of the Lord.

July 3
Psalm 23:1 The Lord is my shepherd; I shall not want. Your shepherd is there beside you to provide all your needs. Rest in the shepherd and follow His lead.

July 4
1 Corinthians 13:6 Do not rejoice in iniquities but rejoice in the Truth. We should not rejoice in sin or wrongdoing, but in the Truth given to us by God.

July 5
Philippians1:6 He who has begun a good work in you will complete it until the day of Jesus Christ. Be encouraged today; God shall complete all that He has promised to do in your life.

July 6
Psalm 12:12 My help comes from the Lord, who made heaven and earth. Every need will be taken care of today, thus says the Lord.

July 7
Psalm 20:1 May the Lord answer you when you are in distress; may the name of God of Jacob protect you. Don't be in distress, God will give His angels charge over you to watch and keep you even when you are sleeping.

July 8
Psalm 20:6 Now I know that the Lord saves His anointed; He answers him from His Holy Heaven with the saving power of His right hand. Hold on to the Lord's powerful hands in this hour; this too shall pass.

July 9
Psalm 27:4 One thing I ask of the Lord, that I may dwell in the house of the Lord all the days of my life, to gaze upon the beauty of the Lord. Go into the Lord's house with a peace; all is well with your soul.

July 10
Psalm 32:1 Blessed is he whose transgressions are forgiven, whose sins are covered. All your sins are covered under the blood. Go forth today as a new creation in the Lord Jesus.

July 11
Psalm 119:63 I am a companion of all who fear you, and of those who keep your precepts. I am your companion when all has forsaken you, come closer; I am drawing you to me to show you how much I love you.

July 12
Lamentation 3:22 *Through the Lord's mercies we are not consumed, because His compassions fail not.* Let the pain and hurts of yesterday go; forgive all. Ask for more mercy to keep you covered during this time of change.

July 13
Matthew 5:8 Blessed are the pure in heart, for they shall see God. Pray to keep a pure heart, you will see the face of God.

July 14
John 11:22 I know that whatever you ask of God, God will give you. Ask according to the Word of God; no good thing will He withhold from you. Ask, it is yours...

July 15
Matthew 18:5 Whoever receives one little child like this in my name receives me. Blessings unto you who serve the little ones with a happy heart.

July 16
Isaiah 43:19 I will even make a way in the wilderness and rivers in the desert. Today your wilderness time is over. Out of your belly will flow living waters to bless others who are in need of what you have to say!

July 17
Psalm 145:14 The Lord upholds all who fall, and raises up all who are bowed down. You have fallen in many areas, but today you shall stand up again for what is right.

July 18
1 John 4:18 There is no fear in love, but perfect love casts out fear, because fear involves torment. Have no fear; give God all your cares of this world, for He cares for you. God wants you to let go and let Him handle this situation.

July19
Psalm 25:4 Show me your ways, O' Lord; teach me your paths. Today, give God your all. He will show you great and mighty things, and take you places you only dream about.

July 20
John 11:22 I know that whatever you ask of God, God will give you. If we have faith and believe that God will do what we ask of Him, He will hear our prayers and grant our requests.

July 21
Romans 8:31 If God is for you, who can be against you? *No one or nothing can stand against who you are in God. I* am with you always.

July 22
Ephesians 5:17 Do not be unwise, but understand what the will of the Lord is…Come into my presence to hear My voice. Stop leaning on your ways, instead, turn your understanding towards God.

July 23
1 Thessalonians 5:18 In everything give thanks, for this is the will of God in Christ Jesus for you. Give God thanks, for your life is in His hands.

July 24
Psalm 35:9 My soul shall be joyful in the Lord; it shall rejoice in His salvation. Give a loud shout unto the Lord who is worthy to be praised.

July 25
1 Peter 5:8 Your adversary the devil walks about like a roaring lion, seeking whom he may devour. You must make a stand against the enemy; stand up and fight, put on your whole armor of God. Victory belongs to you….

July 26
Isaiah 53:5 He was wounded for our transgressions, He was bruised for our iniquities. Today is a new day to be healed of all past hurts, yesterday is gone, this day choose to start a Fresh!

July 27
Ephesians 3:14-15 I bow my knees to the Father of our Lord Jesus Christ, from whom the whole family in heaven and earth is named. Your name has a purpose for you to fulfill. God does the choosing; you are here for such a time as this.

July 28
Psalm 139:23-24 Search me, O God, and know my heart; try me, and know my anxieties…. And lead me in the way everlasting. This day allow God to open your heart and show you what He sees within. He knows all, and He loves you unconditionally.

July 29
Matthew 19:26 …..With God all things are possible. God is the creator of all things, He spoke and so it was. He will give you those things that may seem impossible. Yes, God holds the keys to your possibilities.

July 30
Ezra 8:22 The hand of our God is upon all those for good who seek Him. Pray for God's hand to lead you into more truths of how much He loves you.

July 31
Psalm 37:4 Delight yourself also in the Lord, and He shall give you the desires of your heart. God knows the desires of your heart. Give Him more praise and He will give you more of his power to overcome all things.

Testimony: I encourage you to know our God will bring you through whatever you may be going through. "Nothing is too hard for God, with Him all things are Possible to those who believe that He is who He say He is! Let Go, Let God rule from this day forward. Your Breakthrough is with-in you, speak words of life over yourself and your family, it shall come to pass!

"Break Through"

By: Minister, Timeko Woodward- Huntley

August
Pray without Ceasing
1Thessalonians 5:17

August 1
Psalm 91:1 My dear child, come dwell in the secret place of my presence today. I am waiting on you. Come and sit in God's presence.

August 2
Psalms 95:2 *&100:4* Come before His presence with thanksgiving and make a joyful noise unto Him. Enter His gates with thanksgiving; go into His courts with praise. Give thanks to Him and bless His name.

August 3
Psalm 27:*8*; John 14:13 Lord, my heart has heard You say to come and talk with You. My heart responds, Lord, I am coming. You can ask for anything in His name, and He will do it.

August 4
Colossians 1:9 Lord, I ask that you give me a complete understanding of what you want to do in my life, and I ask that you fill me with spiritual wisdom. Allow God to reveal His plans for your life today.

August 5
Psalm 121:1 & 105:4 I lift up my eyes unto the hills today, for my help comes from God. Lord, I seek your face and ask for your strength. Know that your loving Father is waiting to help you and to give you directions.

August 6
Psalm 62:5-6 Wait quietly before God today, for your hope is in God alone. He is your rock and salvation, a fortress where you will not be shaken.

August 7
Psalm 62:8 Trust, lean on, rely on, and have confidence in Him at all times; pour out your heart before Him. God is a refuge for you. Come to your loving Father in prayer today.

August 8
Proverbs 3:5-6 Put your trust in God always. Trust in the Lord with all your heart; do not depend on your own understanding. Seek His will in all you do, and He will direct your paths.

August 9
Psalm 25:4-5 Show me the path where I should walk, O Lord; point out the right road for me to follow. Lead me by your truth and teach me, for You are the God who saves me. This day I will put my hope in You. Ask the Lord to guide your steps today.

August 10
Psalm 32:8 The Lord says, "I will guide you along the best pathway for your life. I will advise you and watch over you." Take the time to ask for help and allow the Lord to counsel you and help you to make the right decision.

August 11
Psalm 119:18 Father, I ask you to open my eyes today, to see the wonderful truth in Your Word.

August 12
Psalm 119:27 Lord help me to understand the meaning of your commandments, and I will meditate on and talk of Your wondrous works.

August 13
Psalm 119: 33-34 Teach me, O Lord, to follow every one of your principles. Give me the understanding and I will obey your laws; I will put it into practice with all my heart.

August 14
Psalm 86:11 Father, I ask that you teach me Your ways today and I will walk in truth. Soften my heart to reverence Your name.

August 15
Romans 8:26-27 Ask the Holy Spirit to help you to pray. God's word declares that the Holy Spirit comes to our aid and bears us up in our weakness. He interceeds for the saints according to the will of God.

August 16
Psalm 51:10 Father, I ask You that you create within me a clean heart and a right and willing spirit. Lord I ask that You change my heart today and help me to walk in Your perfect will for my life.

August 17
Proverbs 2:3-5 Lord, I come asking you, to give me Your insight and understanding on how to deal with every problem and issue that I am facing. I ask for Your wisdom to make the right decision in every area of my life. Your word declares that I should search for wisdom as I would for lost money

or hidden treasure. Then, I will understand what it means to fear and reverence the Lord.

August 18
Isaiah 41:10 Do not be fearful, for the Lord says "Don't be afraid, for I am with you. Do not be dismayed, for I am Your God. I will strengthen you, I will help you. I will uphold you with my victorious right hand." Cast all of your cares on Him, because He cares for you.

August 19
Psalm 9:3-4 Lord, I ask You to rescue and protect me. He will rescue you from every trap and protect you from the fatal plagues. He will shield you with His wings. He will shelter you with His feathers. His faithful promises are the armor for you and your family.

August 20
Ephesians 3:16-17 Pray that God will give you mighty inner strength through His Holy Spirit, so that by faith Christ may dwell in your heart. Pray also that you may be rooted in God's love.

August 21
2 Corinthians 12:9 I ask you Lord for your enabling grace for Your Word says "My Grace is sufficient for you, for my power is made perfect in your weakness." Walk in God's strength today.

August 22
2 Peter 1:3 Ask God for His divine power in your life. For the Word of God says. "His divine power has given you everything you need for life and godliness through your knowledge of Him, who called you by His own Glory and Goodness."

August 23
Romans 15:13 May the God of hope fill you with all joy and peace as you trust in Him, so that you may overflow with hope by the power of the Holy Spirit.

August 24
Psalm 50:23 Give the Lord thanks today. For the Word of God declares that, he who sacrifices thanks offering honors Me, and he prepares the way so that I may show him the Salvation of God. Whatever you are going through today, give the Lord thanks and watch Him turn your situation around.

August 25
Psalm 68:19 Give God thanks; because He daily loaded you with benefits. He is the God of your salvation. God will meet your every need.

August 26
Psalm 16:11 I praise you today Lord, for showing me the right path to take. I thank you Lord that your Word says "…You will fill me with joy in your presence, with eternal pleasure at your right hand." Come and sit in God's presence and allow Him to fill you with His joy.

August 27
1John 1:9 Confess your sins to God. His word says that if we confess our sins to Him, He is faithful and just to forgive us and to cleanse us from every wrong.

August 28
Psalm 55:22,146:8 & 147:3 Give all of your burdens to the Lord and He will take care of them for you. The Lord opens the eyes of the blind; the Lord lifts the burden off those bent beneath their heavy loads. The Lord heals the broken-hearted, binding up their wounds. Ask Him to set you free today.

August 29
Psalm 25:15; Psalm139:3,16 Keep your eyes on the Lord, for He alone can rescue you from the traps of your enemies. The Lord maps the path ahead of you and tells you where to stop and rest. Every moment He knows where you are. Every moment was laid out before a single day had passed. Put your trust in God today and know that you are safe in His hands.

August 30
II Chronicles 7:14 The word of God say, "If my people who are called by my Name will humble themselves and pray and seek my face and turn from their wicked ways, I will hear from heaven and will forgive their sins and heal their land." It is time to seek God's face and pray.

August 31
John 15:7 Lord, I ask that you help me to abide in you today. T he word of God says."If you will abide in me, and my Word abides in you, you can ask what you will and it shall be done unto you.

My Testimony:
Prayer truly does change things. A few years ago, the Holy Spirit put in my heart to pray for God to bless me with friends that would promote His plans and purpose in my life, and for Him to deliver me and set me free so that I could do His will. I use to be so shy. But because I prayed for God to set me free, he allowed me to meet a friend who shared with me a prayer to break generational cures and set you free. As I prayed to God with all of my heart, I could feel the shackles fall off and set me free. I felt the power of that prayer even as I prayed it. I begin to feel and talk differently and the shyness left me instantly.

God is truly a God who keeps His promises. God is so faithful and He loves you so much. Whatever you need, come to your loving Father in prayer and watch and see Him turn your situation around for you..

"PRAYER CHANGES THINGS"

By: Prophetess, Dianne Causey

September
"Spread your Wings and Soar like the Dove"
Psalm 55:6

I said, "Oh, that I had wings like a dove! I would fly away and be at rest.

September 1
Luke 4:18 He has sent me to heal the brokenhearted, to proclaim liberty to the captives... to set at liberty those who are oppressed. Lord, have your way and heal my broken heart; I am ready for my complete healing.

September 2
2Corinthians 1:3-4 Blessed be the God and Father of our Lord Jesus Christ, the Father of mercies and God of all comfort who comforts us in our entire affliction. Thank you Lord, for your mercies and grace that will comfort me during these times of affliction. Weeping may endure for a night, but I know joy will come in the morning.

September 3
***Proverbs 16:20** He who heeds the Word wisely will find good, and whoever trusts in the Lord, happy is he.* Be happy today. Study His Word day and night, and continue to trust with your whole heart.

September 4
***Jeremiah 18:5-6** The Word of the Lord came to me: O House of Israel, can I not do with you as this potter, so are you in my hand. O House of Israel.* Today give the Lord all of you. He is the potter, you are the clay. You shall be made over again for the Master's use.

September 5
***Psalm 84:11** For the Lord God is a Sun and Shield; the Lord bestows favor and honor, no good thing does He withhold from those whose walk is blameless.* Your blessings are on the way - keep your walk upright before Him. He sees all, and knows all; your time will come sooner than you think.

September 6
***Matthew 7:2** With what judgment you judge, you will be judged.* Stop judging others; you are causing judgment to be passed upon you and your family. Turn it over to the only true and Living God to judge others for the wrongs they have done.

September 7
Ephesians 5:17 Do not be unwise, but understand what the will of the Lord is. Steal away in your secret closet and ask for more understanding of where the Lord is leading you. Don't try anymore to do it your way.

September 8
Hebrew 11:1 Now faith means we are confident of what we hope for; convinced of what we do not see. Take a leap of faith today; keep your inner hope alive.

September 9
John 15:5 ...Without me, you can do nothing. Hold on to the Lord. He is the provider of our strength - without His support and grace, we can accomplish nothing.

September 10
Deuteronomy 7:13 He will love you and bless you and multiply you. You are loved by your Heavenly Father today and forever more.

September 11
John 10:10 I have come that they may have life and that they may have it more abundantly. Enjoy life to its fullest. Take a deep breath and exhale three times.

September 12
2 Peter 2:9 The Lord knows how to deliver the Godly out of temptations. This battle belongs to the Lord; He will deliver you from all the temptations that face you.

September 13
1 Peter 5:7 Cast all your cares upon Him, for He cares for you. The Lord awaits with loving arms for you to come cast everything upon Him. He misses your presence.

September 14
Matthew 18:11 The Son of man has come to save that which was lost. Two thousand years ago you were lost, now you are found, through Jesus Christ.

September 15
Ezekiel 11:19-20 I will give them one heart, and I will put a new spirit within them... that they may walk in my statutes and keep my judgments. Accept you new heart - get up and walk with the Lord today. Your strength is renewed day by day.

September 16
Isaiah 63:16 You, O Lord, are our Father, our Redeemer from everlasting is your name. Worship God's name today and forever more. Worship until you get your breakthrough. Dance and sing unto the Lord, who is worthy to be praised.

September 17
Isaiah 53:4 Surely He has borne our grief's and carried our sorrows. Give thanks unto the Lord who died for us.

September 18
Hebrews 3:4 Every house is built by someone, but He who built all things is God. Lord, help my house to stand firm on your Holy Word.

September 19
Proverbs 3:3 Let not mercy and truth forsake you... write them on the tablet of your heart. Fill your heart with the vision that God has given you; write it down again - you shall have what you write and say.

September 20
1 Corinthians 1:9 God is faithful by whom He called into fellowship of His Son, Jesus Christ our Lord. Praise God, it's time to answer your call to do something for the Lord. We His people need to get into position on the battlefield.

September 21
John 3:27 A man can receive nothing, unless it has been given him from Heaven. You have been waiting and praying, now receive these spiritual blessing from above.

September 22
1 Corinthians 14:33 God is not the author of confusion, but of peace. Open up your mouth and command confusion to depart. Call forth peace on your job, home, car, church - right now, in the name of Jesus!

September 23
Joel 2:25-26 I will restore to you the years that the swarming locust has eaten. You shall... praise the name of the Lord your God. Your latter end shall be greater.

September 24
Romans 8:15 You did not receive the spirit of bondage again to fear, but you received the spirit of adoption by whom we cry out "Abba Father." Cry out to the Lord - tell Him your heart's desires and fears. He is our loving Father, and He will faithfully fulfill His promises to us.

September 25
Psalm 104:1 O' Lord my God, you are very Great; you are clothed with honor and majesty. Clothe me today Lord with more love, and may I feel your majestic glory upon me. I surrender my all; I will love thee forever.

September 26
Romans 8:31 If God is for us, who can be against us? When others leave us, guess what? This is God greatest time to spend with us. Enjoy this time with Him.

September 27
Philippians 4:19 My God shall supply all your needs according to His riches in Glory by Christ Jesus. Yes, all your needs the Lord will supply with His riches.

September 28
Matthew 6:19 If you do not forgive men their trespasses, neither will your Father forgive your trespasses. Forgive all who cause you much disappointment, then you will be free to soar like the Dove.

September 29
John 15:16 I choose you... that you should go and bear fruit. You are chosen by the Highest God. Obey His voice and do His will in the earth.

September 30
James 1:6-7 If any of you lacks wisdom, let him ask God in Faith with no doubting. I come asking you Lord, to speak to my mind. I need your wisdom to know how to live this life that you have given me. Heal my body of sickness, right now, by the Blood of Jesus.

Testimony: With the strength of the Lord Jesus I am able to stand in the storms of life without complaining. I am so thankful for all the Prayer Warriors that's been praying for me. I fully understand that with Our God all things are possible to those who love the Lord. : "This too shall pass..."God is Faithful!.

"With God, You Can Do The Impossible"

By: Prophetess, Meliza Woodward

October
"God is Sufficient"

October 1
Matthew 5:23-24 Therefore if thou bring thy gift to the altar, and there rememberest that thy brother ought against thee; Forgive your brother, so that your gift unto God will be accepted.

October 2
Matthew 7:11 If ye then being evil, know how to give good gifts unto your children, how much more shall your Father which is in heaven give good things to them that ask him. Receive my goodness. Yes, it belongs to you, for I am a good God to those who belong to Me.

October 3
John 4:10 Jesus answered and said unto her, if thou knewest the gift of God, and who it is that saith to thee, give me to drink; thou wouldest have asked of him, and he would have given thee living water. Today, the Lord is giving you His fresh water from heaven. It is yours to receive.

October 4
Romans 1:11 For I long to see you, that I may impart unto you some spiritual gift, to the end ye may be established. Come unto me all who are heavy laden; I long to see and speak to you again. I await.

October 5
Romans 6:23 For the wages of sin is death; but the gift of God is eternal life through Jesus Christ Our Lord. I know all your sins, they come before me, but my gift to you is eternal life. No man can give you what I have already given you.

October 6
Romans 12:6 Having the gift differing according to the grace that is given to us, whether prophecy, let us prophesy according to the proportion of faith. Open your ears and listen to my spoken words. I speak Life, Peace, and most of all Deliverance – they are yours today.

October 7
Deuteronomy 28:12 The LORD shall open unto thee his good treasure. The heaven to give the rain unto thy land in his season, and to bless all the work of thine hand: and thou shalt lend unto many nations, and thou shalt not borrow.

October 8
Matthew 6:21 For where your treasure is, there will your heart be also. Allow your heart to be filled only with doing the will of the Father. No longer your will, but His will.

October 9
Matthew 19:21 Jesus said unto him, if thou wilt be perfect, go and sell that thou hast, and give to the poor, and thou shalt have treasure in heaven: and come and follow me.

October 10
Matthew 6:34 Take therefore no thought for the morrow: for the morrow shall take thought for the things of itself. Sufficient unto the day is the evil thereof.

October 11
1 Corinthians 12:4 Now there are diversities of gifts, but the same spirit. Ask the Lord in your quite time to reveal your gifts and use them for His Glory.

October 12
1 Corinthians 12:31 But covet earnestly the best gifts: and yet shew I unto you a more excellent way. You have the best gifts with-in you, pray for the Lord to help you give birth to all your gifts.

October 13
1 Corinthian 14:1 Follow after charity, and desire spiritual gifts, but rather that ye may prophesy. Today give to someone in need! watch the Lord send you a Blessing.

October 14
2 Corinthians 9:15 Thanks be unto God for his unspeakable gift. Let your light shine before all men.

October 15
Ephesians 2:8 For by grace are ye saved through faith; and that not of yourselves: it is the gift of God.

October 16
1 Timothy 4:14 Neglect not the gift that is in thee, which was given thee by prophecy, with the laying on of the hands of the presbytery. Be free in Jesus to flow in your many gifts.

October 17
2 Timothy 1:6 Wherefore I put thee in remembrance that thou stir up the gift of God, which is in thee by the putting on of my hands. Pray today, ask the Lord to stir up His power...

October 18
James 1:17 Every good gift and every perfect gift is from above, and cometh down from the Father of lights, with whom is no variableness, neither shadow of turning.

October 19
1 Samuel 16:7 But the LORD said unto Samuel, look not on his countenance, or on the height of his stature; because I have refused him: for the LORD seeth not as man seeth; for man looketh on the outward appearance but the LORD looketh on the heart.

October 20
Matthew 5:8 Blessed are the pure in heart; for they shall see God. Tonight the Lord wants to show Himself to you, so you will know whom you serve.

October 21
Matthew 12:35 A good man out of the good treasure of heart bringeth forth good things: and an evil man out of the evil treasure bringeth forth evil things.

October 22
1 Corinthians 2:9 But as it is written, Eye Hath not seen, nor ear heard, neither have entered into the heart of man, the things which God hath prepared for them that love Him.

October 23
Ecclesiastes 8:5 Whoso keepeth the commandment shall feel no evil thing: and a wise man's heart discerneth both time and judgment.

October 24
Philippians 4:7 And the peace of God, which passeth all understanding, shall keep your heart and minds through Christ Jesus.

October 25
1 Peter 3:15 But sanctify the LORD God in your hearts: and be ready always to give an answer to every man that asketh you a reason of the hope that is in you with meekness and fear.

October 26
Jeremiah 8:20 The harvest is past, the summer is ended, and we are not SAVED. It's your time to be saved and filled with My power. Takeheed, the hour is late in the earth.

October 27
Matthew 9:37 Then saith he unto his disciples, the harvest truly is plenteous, but the labourers are few. Go forth, without fear, in whom the Lord has called you to be.

October 28
***Matthew 9:38** Pray ye therefore the LORD of the harvest, that he will send forth labourers into his harvest.* Just say "Yes" to the call. I am the Lord, I will never leave you.

October 29
***John 4:35** Say not yet, there are yet four months, and then cometh harvest? Behold, I say unto you, lift up your eyes, and look on the fields; for they are white already to harvest.*

October 30
***Revelation 14:15** And another angel came out of the temple, crying with a loud voice to him that sat on the cloud, Thrust in thy sickle, and reap; for the harvest of the earth is ripe.* Go into all the earth and Preach the Word.

October 31
***Psalms 139:23** Search me, O God, and know my heart: try me, and know my thoughts.* I surrender my all to you Lord. Get ready for a new change that will last a lifetime.

My Testimony: I am here today because of God's Mercy, On March 18, 2009 I was working on a friend of the family car, with my nephew Perry Sutton, while working under the car, the engine fell from the blocks . I just prayed and felt a hard blow to my head, I felt a strength to lift the engine off me, while trying to get out, the transmission fell, all I felt was a loud crack on the other side of my face. blood start gushing out, I said Lord save me. My nephew ran in the house to get some towels to stop the blood, when he got back , only by the grace of God, I was standing up holding my skin from my head back in place. He drove me to the Douglas County General , I had no fracture to the skull, no broken bones, only 27 staples across my temple with no blood clots, 7 stitches across my right eye, I am a Miracle of God , only 2 weeks later totally healed with no scars as evidence.

"Wash me thoroughly from mine iniquity, and cleanse me from my sins."

By: Pastor, James Theodore Woodward

November
"All Things is Possible with God"
MATTHEW 19:26

November 1
1 Corinthians 6:19 You are not your own
Do you know that you are not your own? We all know that there is no such thing as a private life, or a place to hide in this world for a man or woman.

November 2
John 14:15 Choice of obedience or independence
If you love me, keep my commandments. The lord stresses clearly what we should do concerning being obedient or independent. He does not force us to do it -.we must have the desire and love for His word.

November 3
James 4:8   True authority
Draw nearer to god and he will draw nearer to you. You must give people equal opportunity to respond to the Lord's word. Let it be each individual's responsibility to respond to the Lord's message that you have delivered.

November 4
Matthew 10:27 Listening requires discipline
Whatever I tell you in the dark, speak in the light; and what you hear in the ear, preach on the house tops. There are times when the Lord takes us through certain experiences to teach us to listen and obey. We must stay still and pay attention so that we will be able to share the Lord's word.

November 5
Matthew 6:25 Think twice
......do not worry about your life.... Let the Lord take charge of the battles in your life. No matter what circumstances you come across, our Lord and savior will handle them.

November 6
Philippians 2:1-7 I am ready! Are you ready? Ready to be poured out as an offering?
...*even if I am being poured out as a drink offering on the sacrifice and service of your faith I am glad and rejoice with you all.* Paul was willing to sacrifice his life so that others will place their true faith in Christ. Would you be willing to sacrifice yourself for God's service even if it means being persecuted?

November 7
1 Corinthians 1:1 Greetings of grace. God's calling.
Paul, called to be an apostle of Jesus Christ through the will of god and Sesthenes our brother. If your calling is to preach the Word, and you have been specially chosen as an apostle, your spiritual works should be dedicated to uplifting Jesus Christ.

November 8
Galatians 1:15-16 Leave room for God
But when God, who set me apart from birth and called me by his grace, was pleased to reveal his Son in me so that I might preach him among the Gentiles, I did not consult any man. As servants we are to follow God's instructions without question.

November 9
John 14:9 Time to get intimate with Jesus
Jesus said to him, have I been with you so long, that you still not know me? True friendship is rare in this world. With Jesus the friendship is always there.

November 10
Hebrews 11:8 I will go out without knowing, will you?
….He went out not knowing where he was going. Put your trust in the Lord and let him lead. you.. Take that step of faith - simply walk into it.

November 11
Luke 24:32 The burning heart
….Did not our heart burn within us…? We need to maintain a passion for God's word.

November 12
John 2:24-25 Put God first
Jesus did not commit himself to them…. for he knew what was in man. Put all your trust in God, not in man. If you put your trust in human beings first, the end results would be your own despair and hopelessness.

November 13
Isaiah 2:3 He will teach us His ways, and we shall walk in His paths. Allow the Lord to teach you all things. Today take time to go on a long walk, enjoying what God has made for you to see His wonders.

November 14
1 John 3:23 And this is his command: to believe in the name of his Son, Jesus Christ, and to love one another as he commanded us. Love your enemy today, you shall receive a blessing for praying, and showing agape love to them whom has hurt you..

November 15
John 12:46 I have come as a light into the world, that whoever believes in me should not abide in darkness. Jesus is the light that dwells with-in you, just believe and no darkness can come near you to abide.

November 16
1 John 3:20 Whenever our hearts condemn us, for God is greater than our hearts and knows all things. Whenever your heart condemn you, know your God is greater than your heart emotions which only last for a moment, this too shall pass, with the knowledge that our God knows all and see's all.

November 17
Psalm 31:19 How great is your goodness, which You have laid up for those who fear You. God goodness shall be poured out upon you, all men shall see God's goodness in every area of your life that concerns you and your family.

November 18
Psalm 84:11 The Lord will give Grace and Glory. No good thing will He withhold from those who walk uprightly. My grace and glory will be revealed in your life, just trust my timing, you will see how precious you are to me.

November 19
Psalm 42:8 In the night His song shall be with me as a prayer to the God of my life. Listen to the music of your heart, open your mouth and sing a new melody unto me. Today your song will be your breakthrough to be heard through-out Eternity.

November 20
Psalm 119:63 I am a companion of all who fear you, and of those who keep your precepts.
I am your God, look-up, I am here with you, I feel the pain, hurts and trials that you are facing, this is only a test to strengthen you for the Journey ahead.

November 21
Romans 13:2 Let us cast off the works of darkness, and let us put on the armor of light. Let go of your past of darkness, don't look back, walk upright with the Armor of light that I have bestowed upon you, many will follow after the Light as you walk before men in my Glory!

November 22
Psalm 24:1 The earth is the Lord's, and all its fullness, the world and those who dwell therein. Seek no longer to fulfill your own desires, but fulfill my purpose in the earth. Then you will find my perfect peace you been searching for...

November 23
Philippians 4:4 Rejoice in the Lord always, again I say rejoice! Make a joyful noise unto me, I await to hear from you more each day. I want to give you unspeakable joy, that no man can give or take away.

November 24
Mark 9:24 I believe; help my unbelief. I am here for you, just ask and believe it is yours today by having faith in who I am in your life. "Take a deep breath" Just believe it's Done...

November 25
Nehemiah 8:10 The Joy of the Lord is your Strength. When you feel weak, speak forth my joy to spring up from with-in, this will strengthen you to run on and finish the race that is set before you.

November 26
1Kings 8:61 Let you heart therefore be loyal to the Lord our God. Now, is the time to stop being pleasing and loyal to men, but know the hour is late, be committed unto the Lord your God.

November 27
Psalm 126:5 Those who sow in tears shall reap in Joy. Your time has come to reap your harvest of much joy, enjoy this time of your life with family and those who love you with Godly love, no conditions attach.

November 28
Revelation 17:14 He is Lord of Lords, and King of Kings. There is no lord or god beside me, who love you, for whom you have become in me. Trust and lean on me to bring you through .

November 29
Psalm 104:24   O Lord, how manifold are your works! In wisdom you have made them all. Look in the mirror today, what do you see? You are the manifold of my beauty , I created in the earth for all men to see.

November 30
Exodus 13:21   And the Lord went before them…. to lead the way. Your way has already be cleared before the foundation of the earth, go forth in your overcoming faith.

By: Teacher, Carolyn James

December
"Keep the Faith, Keep on Praying"

December 1
Psalms 30:5 Weeping may endure for a night, but joy comes in the morning. When dealing with controversy, know that at the end God will grant you unspeakable peace. Your reward is in knowing your earthly pain will pass away and having the assurance that heaven is forever.

December 2
1 Samuel 7:12 Samuel took a stone...and called its name Ebenezer, saying, "Thus far the Lord has helped us." If you are dealing with a battle that seems too hard to handle, turn it over to the Lord and allow him to fight it for you. Take inventory of your life and all the times God has brought you through.

December 3
Job 19:25 I know that my Redeemer lives. God manifested Himself to us in the form of Jesus Christ. After He was crucified He rose on the third day with all power in His hand. Man crucified Him, God raised Him, and today we have the victory through His resurrection.

December 4
Luke 2:1 For unto you is born this day in the city of David a Savior, which is Christ the Lord. Man brought sin into the world and woman brought a holy man into the world to give us redemption. Jesus was born so that we might have life abundantly.

December 5
Psalms 46:10 Be still, and know that I am God. God wants us to take time from the hustle and bustle of life to spend time with him. Go into your secret place and allow God to give you rest.

December 6
Matthew 22:39 You shall love your neighbor as yourself. God requires us to love everyone, not just the ones that treat us right. How can you love God whom you cannot see and not love your neighbor, the one you can see? Take time today to tell someone you love them. Even if, in your sight, they do not deserve it.

December 7
2 Corinthians 5:17 If anyone is in Christ, he is a new creation; old things have passed away; behold, all things have become new. What can others see in you that will let them know you are a new creature? When you accept Christ as your Lord and Savior, you must put away the things of this world and allow the Holy Spirit to guide you.

December 8
Proverbs 10:19 He who restrains his lips is wise. Every uttered word from your mouth should be sounds of joy and adoration, not words that will tear down the body of Christ. Stop, think, and listen to the Holy Spirit before you speak. If necessary, ask God to speak for you.

December 9
James 4:7 Submit yourselves therefore to God. Resist the devil, and he will flee from you. You have the power through Jesus Christ to rebuke the devil. Do not let Satan control your life; accept the Lord as your Savior and he will abide in you as you abide in him.

December 10
Genesis 13:2 And Abram was very rich in cattle, in silver, and in gold. Just as God blessed Abram, he will do the same for you if you follow his commandments and not faint. Do not stray from God's word; in everything give thanks unto the Lord.

December 11
Malachi 3:8 Will a man rob God? Yet ye have robbed me. But ye say, Wherein have we robbed thee? In tithes and offerings. In order for God to release his full blessings upon us, we must bless him by honoring his commandment to tithe. When you hold on to that which God has blessed you with, it makes it impossible for new blessings to come through.

December 12
Luke 8:8 And other fell on good ground, and sprang up, and bear fruit a hundredfold. And when he had said these things, he cried. He that hath ears to hear let him hear. When you sew good seeds into your spiritual body, you will reap a harvest full of blessing that you can share with others. However, it must start with you getting to know the Lord. What type of seed are you planting?

December 13
Matthew 6:24 No one can serve two masters for either he will hate the one and love the other, or else he will be loyal to the one and despise the other. You cannot serve God and mammon. God requires all of you, not just the part that you desire for him to have. In order to have a complete and lasting relationship with God, you must put away the things of this world and allow God to be first in your life.

December 14
Mark 10:51 So Jesus answered and said to him, "What do you want Me to do for you?" The blind man said to Him, Rabboni, that I may receive my sight." Whatever it is that you seek from Jesus, ask and believe in his name that it will be granted. We have not because we ask not. Ask knowing that your father will supply *"all"* of your needs according to his riches in glory.

December 15
2 Samuel 7:1 Now it came to pass when the king was dwelling in his house, and the Lord had given him rest from all his enemies all around. When your enemies come up against you, seek refuge in the Lord and allow him to hide you in the secret places of his tabernacle. Seek the face of the Lord and he will give you rest from your enemies.

December 16
Psalm27:14 Wait on the Lord; be of good courage, and he shall strengthen thine heart: wait, I say, on the Lord. When all else fails, place your cares in the hands of God and he will work it out for you. Be patient and want for nothing, God is still in control, he is waiting on you. Go boldly before his throne with a humble heart and watch him work a miracle in your life.

December 17
Habakkuk 2:3 For the vision is yet for an appointed time: But at the end it will speak and it will not lie. Though it tarries, wait for it: Because it will surely come, It will not tarry. God promised us eternal rest in his kingdom. When times are hard and friends are few, rest assured that what God has promised will come to pass. Be patient and watch the Lord's hand do his work.

December 18
John 3:3 Jesus answered and said to him, "Most assuredly, I say to you, unless one is born again, he cannot see the kingdom of God." Being born again requires a spiritual awakening which occurs when we believe in the Lord. In order to inherit the kingdom that God had promised us, you must renew your spiritual being.

December 19
Genesis 2:18 And the Lord God said, "It is not good that man should be alone: I will make him a helper comparable to him." If God gives us someone as a special gift to make us whole, they ought to be cherished and protected for a lifetime. God did not desire for man to be alone. Seek God and he shall supply you with a helper.

December 20
2 Samuel 11:2 Then it happened one evening that David arose from his bed and walked on the roof of the king's house. And from the roof he saw a woman bathing, and the woman was very Beautiful to behold. We must all recognize our roof where we become susceptible to temptation: Is there a restlessness which is causing us to drift from God? Are we spending time and energy on activities, in places or conversations, we know are not honoring to God? Let's remain in His presences and ask God to open our eyes to the vulnerable areas of our life; let's commit to walk the path of purity and stay off the roof!

December 21
Psalm 46:10 Be still, and know that I am God: I will be exalted among the nations, I will be exalted in the earth! We are all given a gift of the same 24 hours in every day. Yet, most of us generally try to put far too much into this precious time. For this reason, God gives us a gentle reminder - actually, He gives us a firm command - which is to stand still.

December 22
Hebrews 11:1 Now faith is the substance of things hoped for, the evidence of things not seen. Worshiping God means we must believe in him even though we cannot see him. We do not see the wind blow, but we know it is there because we feel it. When was the last time you felt the presence of God?

December 23
Daniel 3:25 Look! He answered, "I see four men loose, walking in the midst of the fire: and they are not hurt, and the form of the fourth is like the Son of God." The fires in our life WILL come. The heat will seem intense, but we must not fear or abandon what we know to be true. Our faith is ALWAYS refined and made stronger by fire; the testing of your faith develops perseverance.

December 24
Luke 14:27 And whoever does not bear his cross and come after Me cannot be My disciple. We are called to love God with ALL our heart, soul, mind, and strength and in doing so God will supply the rest. If we want to dwell with God, we must surrender self.

****************December 25** **************
James 4:10 Humble yourselves in the sight of the Lord, and he shall lift you up. When you feel down and out, lift your head up to heaven knowing that the Lord will renew your strength. Go to the father as a little child and allow him to comfort you.

December 26
Amos 7:7 Thus he showed me: Behold, the Lord stood on a wall made with a plumb line, with a plumb line in His hand. God has established clear guidelines and preserved them within His Word. We cannot continue to build using the world's system of values as our reference. This is a standard in constant change, sinking deeper and deeper into the slimy pit. If we do not change, we will sink with it. This should NOT be our chosen path!!

December 27
John 12:32   And I, if I am lifted up from the earth will draw all men unto me. When Jesus was "lifted up" on the cross and died for our sin, He provided the way back to the Father - the way to become His disciple. He drew us to Himself so we could be forgiven and stand in the presence of God.

December 28
Philippians 4:6   Be anxious for nothing, but in everything by prayer and supplication, with thanksgiving, let your requests be made known to God. Give God the thanks for all that he hath provided. When the praises goes up, the blessings come down. Thank God for all that you have no matter how great or how small.

December 29
Psalms: 111:10   The fear of the Lord is the beginning of wisdom: a good understanding have all they that do his commandments: his praise endureth for ever. Fear the Lord and he will provide you wisdom beyond compare. Keep his commandments and he will richly bless you and your offspring's for generations to come.

December 30
***John 16:33** These things I have spoken to you, that in Me you may have peace. In the world you will have tribulation: but be of good cheer, I have overcome the world.* Jesus came to conquer sin and death through His sacrifice on the cross. When we come to Him in faith and receive the transforming gift of His Spirit, we ought to keep this truth at the front of ALL our thoughts: the battle has already been won!

December 31
***Romans 10:10** For with the heart one believes unto righteousness, and with the mouth confession is made unto salvation.* Believing in our heart means much more than simply knowing the story. It means a belief which pumps through every part of our body and gives us life.

Testimony:

The thing that I'm most grateful for is the favor that God showed me when he afforded me the opportunity of a lifetime. I wanted to visit Africa and possibly do missionary work over there. In October 2008 God along with the assistance of Pastor Meliza made my dream a reality. When I stepped off the plane in Africa all of my prayers were answered. I saw wonders in Africa that I never dreamed would ever come true, if God does not answer another prayer, I will be satisfied because he gave me the desire of my heart. I thank him and Pastor Meliza for allowing me the chance to fellowship with people from the mother-land.

"Pray without Ceasing"

By: Evangelist, Shirley Hayden-Spann

CONCLUSION
" Special Blessing Released "

In Conclusion, I pray a prayer of release upon your life and your family. I bind up all generational curses that have been in your family for 4 generation to lose you and your family right now, in the name of Jesus.

I pray no more generational curses shall come back to re-attach again, I decree in the name of Jesus you and your family shall walk in your new Victory, free from all the sins of your forefathers. Today dawns a new day of hope, peace, strength, and most of all that you will have a closer walk with your Heavenly Father, Jesus Christ the Son, and the Holy Spirit your Comforter. You are released to become all that the Lord has created you to become. Amen!

Repeat this Prayer: Release shall come into my life, I will never turn back to who I used to be, I will not let anyone speak over my life anymore doubt, fear, or bondage of "whata, coulda, shoulda," I, shall Go forth Enjoying my new beginnings. I shall Stand on the Promises of God 366 days a year. Reading this book has allowed me to travel a journey that has given me a better understanding of God's Promises. I know all my prayers shall come to pass according to God's Word. I shall stay Faithful, and He will be Faithful to those who belongs to Him. I shall never doubt my Heavenly Father Love for me and my family. Amen!

Message from the Author: What a Blessing to have you read this Daily Word 366 days of the year. Thanks you for the support on our first book to be published by the leading of the Holy Spirit. " Whispers of Faith Publishing Company" is here to help you unfold your stories for the world to see and hear. This is just the beginning for us, the Lord has much more for us all, that will be revealed in God's timing to reach the Nations.

A Special Prayer for your family, friends, and enemies. Cast all your cares of this world upon the Lord, for He Cares for you. *I pray every need will be fulfilled in your life by the Blood of Jesus Christ.* Get Ready to receive all that the Lord has for you and your family today, tomorrow, and forever. Expect daily Benefits to be given unto you.

Spoken Prophecy: Every reader of this book, shall receive a Financial blessing for buying this book. Today as you close this year out, expect next year to become the Years of Open Doors from the Lord. What the Lord has in store for your family; no weapon formed against you shall prosper or stop the Lord from completing the works that is with-in you. Breakthrough belongs to you! Get- up right where you are, do a **VICTORY DANCE..... Shout with a loud voice, NOW IT'S MY TIME, MY TURN, Praise the Lord Jesus Christ for your Freedom!!!**

Daughter of the Zion, Meliza

Sweet Auburn Film Festival 2008
"Audience Award"
Agape Award Winning Film 2008
"Best Film"

DVD for sale $10.00 Love Offering or any Donations will be accepted
Deliverance in the House" will bring change into your homes, laughter, and hope for every family. This movie is about issues we deal with everyday, those things we keep hidden in secret feed the bondage in our lives'... But the Truth Sets Us FREE!!!

"Deliverance in the House"
Written by: Prophetess, Meliza Fleming-Woodward
&
Jermaine Ka'Mell

"Whispers of Faith Publishing Company" is a Division of TakeHeed Ministry & Productions

Order on Line: "Standing on the Promises" $9.99
E-mail: whispersoffaith@yahoo.com
E-mail: takeheed333@yahoo.com
place order by Phone: 404-554-5027

" IT"S YOUR TIME TO OPEN UP AND BLOOM RIGHT WHERE YOU ARE"!

Special Graphic: Bobby M Peoples
Bobby@tpn1.com or visit www.TPN1.com
Maxine Hopkins
www.maxinehopkinsministries.org

" God Bless you"

Standing on God's Word: Notes

Promises to Wait On: Notes

Faith Believing: Notes

Journal of Changes: Notes

Made in the USA
Columbia, SC
22 September 2022